Safe work in confined spaces

Confined Spaces Regulations 1997

APPROVED CODE OF PRACTICE, REGULATIONS AND GUIDANCE

L101

HSE BOOKS

© Crown copyright 1997
Applications for reproduction should be made in writing to:
Copyright Unit, Her Majesty's Stationery Office,
St Clements House, 2-16 Colegate, Norwich NR3 1BQ

First published 1997

ISBN 0 7176 1405 0

This Code has been approved by the Health and
Safety Commission, with the consent of the
Secretary of State. It gives practical advice on how to
comply with the law. If you follow the advice you
will be doing enough to comply with the law in
respect of those specific matters on which the Code
gives advice. You may use alternative methods to
those set out in the Code in order to comply with the
law. However, the Code has a special legal status. If
you are prosecuted for breach of health and safety
law, and it is proved that you did not follow the
relevant provisions of the Code, you will need to
show that you have complied with the law in some
other way or a court will find you at fault.

This Approved Code of Practice also contains
guidance. This guidance is issued by the Health and
Safety Commission. Following the guidance is not
compulsory and you are free to take other action.
But if you do follow the guidance you will normally
be doing enough to comply with the law. Health and
Safety inspectors seek to secure compliance with the
law and may refer to this guidance as illustrating
good practice.

Contents

By virtue of section 16(1) of the Health and Safety at Work etc Act 1974, and with the consent of the Secretary of State for Environment, Transport and the Regions, the Health and Safety Commission has on 31 July 1997 approved the Code of Practice entitled *Safe work in confined spaces*.

The Code of Practice is approved for the purposes of providing practical guidance with respect to the requirements of the Confined Spaces Regulations 1997 (SI 1997 No 1713) and with respect to sections 2-4, 6 and 7 of the Health and Safety at Work etc Act 1974, the Management of Health and Safety at Work Regulations 1992 (SI 1992 No 2051), the Control of Substances Hazardous to Health Regulations 1994 (SI 1994 No 3246), the Personal Protective Equipment at Work Regulations 1992 (SI 1992 No 2966), and the Provision and Use of Work Equipment Regulations 1992 (SI 1992 No 2932). The Code of Practice comes into force on 28 January 1998.

Reference in this Code of Practice to another document does not imply approval by the Health and Safety Commission of that document except to the extent necessary to give effect to this Code of Practice.

Signed

ROSEMARY BANNER
Secretary to the Health and Safety Commission

31 July 1997

1   The Confined Spaces Regulations 1997 were made under the Health and Safety at Work etc Act (HSW Act) 1974 and came into force on 28 January 1998. The Regulations apply in all premises and work situations in Great Britain subject to the HSW Act, with the exception of diving operations and below ground in a mine (there is specific legislation dealing with confined spaces in these cases). The Regulations also extend outside Great Britain in a very limited number of cases (see paragraph 16). The full text of the Confined Spaces Regulations 1997 (SI 1997 No 1713) is available from HMSO.

2   This publication contains an Approved Code of Practice (ACOP) and guidance on the duties in the Confined Spaces Regulations which are applicable across all industry sectors and which apply to working in confined spaces but which do not apply offshore. This publication also gives guidance on the duties in other Regulations where they apply to work in confined spaces. These existing Regulations are principally the Management of Health and Safety at Work Regulations 1992 (Management Regulations), the Control of Substances Hazardous to Health Regulations 1994 (COSHH), the Personal Protective Equipment at Work Regulations 1992, the Provision and Use of Work Equipment Regulations 1992, the Control of Lead at Work Regulations 1980, and the Control of Asbestos at Work 1987. There are separate and specific HSE publications providing guidance on each of these Regulations, as well as publications concerned with specific hazards and equipment (see Appendix 3 for details).

3   In this publication, the Confined Spaces Regulations 1997 are shown in *italic* type. The Approved Code of Practice, which has the status described on page ii, is shown in **bold** type. The remaining text, in medium type, is additional guidance on the subject.

4   This Approved Code of Practice and guidance have been prepared by the Health and Safety Executive (HSE) for the Health and Safety Commission (HSC) after widespread consultation with industry.

MEANING OF 'CONFINED SPACE'

Confined Spaces Regulations 1997

Citation, commencement and interpretation

(1)   These regulations may be cited as the Confined Spaces Regulations 1997 and shall come into force on 28th January 1998.

(2)   In these Regulations, unless the context otherwise requires -

"confined space" means any place, including any chamber, tank, vat, silo, pit, trench, pipe, sewer, flue, well or other similar space in which, by virtue of its enclosed nature, there arises a reasonably foreseeable specified risk;

"diving operation" has the meaning assigned thereto by regulation 2(1) of the Diving Operations at Work Regulations 1981[(a)];

"free flowing solid" means any substance consisting of solid particles and which is of, or is capable of being in, a flowing or running consistency, and includes flour, grain, sugar, sand or other similar material;

(a)   SI 1981/399; relevant amending instrument is SI 1990/996.

"mine" has the meaning assigned thereto by section 180 of the Mines and Quarries Act 1954[b];

"specified risk" means a risk of -

(a)   *serious injury to any person at work arising from a fire or explosion;*

(b)   *without prejudice to paragraph (a) -*

(i)   *the loss of consciousness of any person at work arising from an increase in body temperature;*

(ii)   *the loss of consciousness or asphyxiation of any person at work arising from gas, fume, vapour or the lack of oxygen;*

(c)   *the drowning of any person at work arising from an increase in the level of liquid; or*

(d)   *the asphyxiation of any person at work arising from a free flowing solid or the inability to reach a respirable environment due to entrapment by a free flowing solid;*

"system of work" includes the provision of suitable equipment which is in good working order.

(b)   *1954 c.70; section 180 was modified by paragraph 3 of Part 1 of Schedule 2 to SI 1974/2013 and by Schedule 3, Part II of SI 1993/1897.*

5   Under these regulations a 'confined space' has two defining features. Firstly, it is a place which is substantially (though not always entirely) enclosed and, secondly, there will be a reasonably foreseeable risk of serious injury from hazardous substances or conditions within the space or nearby.

6   Some confined spaces are fairly easy to identify, for example, closed tanks, vessels and sewers. Others are less obvious but may be equally dangerous, for example, open-topped tanks and vats, closed and unventilated or inadequately ventilated rooms and silos, or constructions that become confined spaces during their manufacture.

7   Some places which fall within the definition of a confined space may be so only occasionally, perhaps due to the type of work to be undertaken, for example, a room during spray painting. Also, a confined space may not necessarily be enclosed on all sides. Some confined spaces, for example vats, silos and ships' holds, may have open tops. Places not usually considered to be confined spaces may become confined spaces because of a change in the condition inside or a change in the degree of enclosure or confinement, which may occur intermittently.

8   In addition to the places referred to in regulation 1(2), the expression 'confined space' may also refer to the following examples and other similar places: ducts, vessels, culverts, tunnels, boreholes, bored piles, manholes, shafts, excavations, sumps, inspection pits, cofferdams, freight containers, ship cargo holds/tanks, ballast tanks, double bottoms, ships' engine rooms, buildings, building voids, some enclosed rooms (particularly plant rooms) and compartments within them, including some cellars, enclosures for the purpose of asbestos removal, and interiors of machines, plant or vehicles. However, application of the Regulations in any of these places will depend on the presence of a reasonably foreseeable risk of serious injury.

The hazards

9   The hazards that the Confined Spaces Regulations address arise through the combination of the confined nature of the place of work and the possible

presence of substances or conditions which, taken together, could increase the risk to the safety or health of people. Remember that a hazard can be introduced to a substantially enclosed space that otherwise would be safe. The most likely hazards are as follows:

- **_Flammable substances and oxygen enrichment_**

    A risk of fire or an explosion can arise from the presence of flammable substances. There can also be a risk of fire and explosion from an excess of oxygen in the atmosphere, for example, caused by a leak from an oxygen cylinder forming part of welding equipment. There is also a risk of explosion from the ignition of airborne flammable contaminants. A fire or explosion can also be caused by leaks from adjoining plant or processes that have not been effectively isolated.

- **_Toxic gas, fume or vapour_**

    Fume may remain from previous processing or as a result of previous storage, or arise from sludge or other deposits disturbed, for example during cleaning. Hydrocarbon vapour may also be present under scale even after cleaning. Fume may also enter the space from adjoining plant that has not been effectively isolated. Gas and fume can build up in sewers, manholes, contaminated ground or leak from behind vessel linings, rubber, lead, brick etc. Fume and vapour can also be produced by work inside the confined space, for example, welding, flame cutting, lead lining, brush and spray painting, or moulding using glass reinforced plastics, use of adhesives or solvents, or from the products of combustion. They can also occur inside a compartment or space by hot work taking place on the exterior surfaces or enter the space from equipment in use outside the space, such as exhaust fume from mobile plant, especially on construction sites. Plant failure can also cause problems: for example, by the build-up of ammonia if refrigeration plant fails or the potential for accumulation of carbon dioxide in pub cellars following leaks from compressed gas cylinders.

- **_Oxygen deficiency_**

    Oxygen deficiency may result from, for example:

    - purging of the confined space with an inert gas to remove flammable or toxic gas, fume, vapour or aerosols;

    - naturally occurring biological processes consuming oxygen, which can occur in sewers, storage tanks, storm water drains, wells etc. Similarly gases can be produced as a result of fermentation in sealed silos where crops have been or are being stored; in fermentation vessels in brewing; or in cargo holds caused by the carriage of timber or timber products, steel turnings or swarf, vegetable products, grain, coal etc;

    - leaving a vessel completely closed for some time (particularly one constructed of steel) since the process of rust formation on the inside surface consumes oxygen. Newly fabricated or shot blasted carbon steel vessels are especially vulnerable to rusting, particularly those with a large surface area, for example, heat exchangers, separators, filters etc;

    - the risk of increased levels of carbon dioxide from limestone chippings associated with drainage operations when they get wet;

3

– burning operations and work such as welding and grinding which consume oxygen;

– displacement of air during pipe freezing, for example, with liquid nitrogen;

– a gradual depletion of oxygen as workers breathe in confined spaces and where provision of replacement air is inadequate.

- *The ingress or presence of liquids*

   Liquids can flow into the confined space and lead to drowning and other serious injury depending on the nature of the liquids such as their corrosivity or toxicity.

- *Solid materials which can flow*

   Free flowing solids can submerge a person, preventing breathing. Materials which create this hazard include grain, sugar, flour, sand, coal-dust and other substances in granular or powder form.

- *Presence of excessive heat*

   This can lead to a dangerous rise in core body temperature and can be made worse as a result of personal protective equipment being worn. In extreme cases heat stroke and unconsciousness can result. A slower heat build-up in the body can cause heat stress, and if action is not taken to cool the body there is also a risk of heat stroke and unconsciousness. This can occur where work in hot conditions is being undertaken in a confined space or where, for example, boilers or furnaces have not been allowed sufficient time to cool before people are allowed to enter to undertake maintenance work, or where equipment has been steam cleaned to remove hydrocarbons.

10   Other hazards can be found when entering or working in confined spaces but they are not the specific concern of these Regulations, the Approved Code of Practice or this Guidance. This is because these hazards are not unique to confined spaces working. The precautions for dealing with hazards such as: electricity; mechanical equipment; noise; dust; and working space, are not specifically dealt with in the Confined Space Regulations, the Approved Code of Practice or this Guidance. Where these hazards are present in a confined space the precautions will almost always be more extensive than where they appear outside the confined space simply because of the enclosed nature of the space.

11   Specific regulations and supporting guidance already deal with many of these other hazards, for example:

- Electricity at Work Regulations 1989

- Provision and Use of Work Equipment Regulations 1992

- Noise at Work Regulations 1989

- Workplace (Health, Safety and Welfare) Regulations 1992

- Control of Lead at Work Regulations 1980

- Control of Asbestos at Work Regulations 1987.

The Control of Substances Hazardous to Health Regulations 1994 (COSHH) also apply to all substances hazardous to health (other than lead or asbestos), such as toxic fume and injurious dust. The Ionising Radiation Regulations 1985 may apply where radon gas can accumulate in confined spaces, for example, sewers, and where industrial radiography is used to look at, for example, the integrity of welds in vessels (see Appendix 3).

APPLICATION OF THE REGULATIONS

Confined Spaces Regulations 1997

Regulation 2

Disapplication of Regulations

Regulation

These Regulations shall not apply to or in relation to -

(a) the master or crew of a sea-going ship or to the employer of such persons in respect of the normal ship-board activities carried out solely by a ship's crew under the direction of the master; or

(b) any place below ground in a mine; or

(c) any diving operation to and in relation to which the Diving Operations at Work Regulations 1981 apply by virtue of regulation 3 of those Regulations.

Regulation 8

Extension outside Great Britain

Regulation

These Regulations shall, subject to regulation 2 above, apply to and in relation to the premises and activities outside Great Britain to which sections 1 to 59 and 80 of the 1974 Act apply by virtue of paragraphs (a), (b), (d) and (e) of article 8 of the Health and Safety at Work etc Act 1974 (Application Outside Great Britain) Order 1995[(a)] as they apply within Great Britain but they shall not apply in any case where at the relevant time article 4, 5, 6 or 7 of the said Order applies.

(a)   SI 1995/263.

Guidance

12   The Confined Spaces Regulations apply in all premises and work situations subject to the HSW Act, with the exception of diving operations, and below ground in a mine. Specific legislation deals with confined spaces in these cases, and guidance is available (see Appendix 3). In addition the Regulations do not apply to the master or crew of a sea-going ship or to the employer of such persons in respect of the normal ship-board activities carried out solely by a ship's crew under the direction of the master.

ACOP

13   **Where an operation involves a ship's crew and shoreside workers working together aboard ship, the provisions will apply, thereby imposing duties on masters, crew and their employers, as well as the shoreside workers involved and their employers. They will need to co-operate so far as is necessary to ensure that their duties in relation to these matters are discharged, agreeing procedures and establishing who is in overall control as required under regulation 9 of the Management Regulations.**

ACOP

14   The Confined Spaces Regulations also revoke regulations 48-52 and 54 of the Shipbuilding and Ship-repairing Regulations 1960, which deal with work in confined spaces. However, regulations 59-66 of the Shipbuilding and Ship-repairing Regulations deal with hot-work and may also involve work in confined spaces. By complying with the requirements of regulations 59-66 in full, you will be deemed to have fully complied with the requirements of the Confined Spaces Regulations, until such time as regulations 59-66 have been revoked.

15   When entering compression chambers or diving bells provided for the support of diving operations to conduct pre- and post-diving procedures, setting-to work (ie commissioning equipment), or maintenance procedures, the Confined Spaces Regulations will apply because these activities are not defined as diving operations under the Diving Operations at Work Regulations 1981.

Guidance

16   The Regulations also extend outside Great Britain in a limited number of cases where the HSW Act applies by virtue of paragraphs (a), (b), (d) and (e) of article 8 of the Health and Safety at Work etc Act 1974 (Application Outside Great Britain) Order 1995.

ACOP

17   Offshore installations are not specifically covered by the Confined Spaces Regulations (and hence this Code). The Confined Spaces Regulations would apply to certain activities aboard installations 'stacked' out of use in territorial waters, which are not defined as 'offshore installations', such as the activities of shore-based workers undertaking repair, maintenance or cleaning.

DUTIES UNDER THE REGULATIONS

Confined Spaces Regulations 1997

Regulation 3

Persons upon whom duties are imposed by these Regulations

Regulation

(1)   Every employer shall -

(a)   ensure compliance with the provisions of these Regulations in respect of any work carried out by his employees; and

(b)   ensure compliance, so far as is reasonably practicable, with the provisions of these Regulations in respect of any work carried out by persons other than his employees insofar as the provisions relate to matters which are within his control.

(2)   Every self-employed person shall -

(a)   comply with the provisions of these Regulations in respect of his own work; and

(b)   ensure compliance, so far as is reasonably practicable, with the provisions of these Regulations in respect of any work carried out by other persons insofar as the provisions relate to matters which are within his control.

18 Duties to comply with the Regulations are placed on:

- **employers in respect of work carried out by their own employees and work carried out by any other person (eg contractors) insofar as that work is to any extent under the employers' control; and**

- **the self-employed in respect of their own work and work carried out by any other person insofar as that work is to any extent under the control of the self-employed.**

19 **Where employers or the self-employed have duties in relation to people at work who are not their employees then the duty is to do what is 'reasonably practicable' in the circumstances. In many cases, the employer or self-employed will need to liaise and co-operate with others (eg other employers) to agree the respective responsibilities in terms of the regulations and duties. It is also necessary to take all reasonably practicable steps to engage competent contractors. In this way, those in control can be clear about what they can reasonably do to ensure that those undertaking the work in the confined space comply with these and other relevant regulations.**

RISK ASSESSMENT

The Management of Health and Safety at Work Regulations 1992: regulation 3 (see Appendix 1)

20 The Management of Health and Safety at Work Regulations 1992 apply across all industries and all work activities. The principal duty, regulation 3 (see Appendix 1), requires all employers and self-employed persons to identify the measures they need to take by means of a suitable and sufficient assessment of all risks to workers and any others who may be affected by their work activities (insignificant risks can be ignored). Employers with five or more employees are required to record the significant findings of the assessment. The Approved Code of Practice *Management of Health and Safety at Work* provides further details (see Appendix 3).

21 In accordance with regulation 4(1) of The Confined Spaces Regulations 1997, the priority when carrying out a risk assessment is to identify the measures needed so that work in confined spaces can be avoided. If, in the light of the risks identified, it cannot be considered reasonably practicable to carry out the work without entering the confined space, then it is necessary to determine what measures need to be taken to secure a safe system for working within the confined space in accordance with regulation 4(2). The risk assessment will help identify the necessary precautions to be included in the safe system of work, and is described in more detail in paragraph 36.

22 (a) **If it is not reasonably practicable to prevent work in a confined space the employer or the self-employed will need to assess the risks connected with entering or working in the space. The assessment will need to identify the risks to those entering or working there, and also any others, for example, other workers including contractors and the general public in the vicinity who could be affected by the work to be undertaken. Assessment upon which a safe system of work is to be based must be carried out by those competent to do so.**

(b) **A competent person for these purposes will be someone with sufficient experience of, and familiarity with, the relevant** processes, plant and equipment so that they understand the risks involved and can devise necessary precautions to meet the requirements of the Confined Space Regulations. In complex cases more than one person may be needed to conduct assessment of risks relating to specific required areas of expertise.

23 Where a number of confined spaces (eg sewers or manholes) are broadly the same, in terms of the conditions and the activities being carried out, and if the risks and measures to deal with them are the same, it may be possible to devise a 'model' or generic risk assessment covering them all. Any differences in particular cases that would alter the conclusions of the model risk assessment must be identified. Failure to include relevant information in the risk assessment could lead to inadequate precautions in the subsequent system of work.

24 When carrying out an assessment, you should make use of all information available about the confined space. For example, there may be information from engineering drawings, working plans or about relevant soil or geological conditions. Assess this information in conjunction with information on any processes that have already taken place or will take place in the course of the work to be undertaken and which could affect the condition of the confined space. Information relevant to emergency arrangements are dealt with at paragraph 80.

25 Employees and their representatives should be consulted when assessing the risks connected with entering or working in a confined space.

26 Give particular attention to situations where the work circumstances are changing, for example at construction sites or steel fabrications, or where there are temporary workers who are likely to have limited knowledge of the conditions and dangers in the confined space.

Factors to be assessed

27 (a) You should assess the general condition of the confined space to identify what might be present or not present, and cause a problem: for example, is the concentration of oxygen normal? Any records relating to the confined space should be checked for relevant information. Consideration should be given to:

● *Previous contents*

Information about any substances previously held, however briefly, in the confined space, will give an indication of what kind of hazard may be expected, for example, toxic or flammable gases, etc. Fires and explosions have been caused by ignition of substances thought to have been 'removed' some considerable time before, but which were, in fact, still present.

● *Residues*

Dangers may arise from chemical residues or scale, rust, sludge or other residues in a confined space. For example, dangerous gas, fume or vapour can be released when scale, sludge or animal slurry is disturbed. Where there are residues, safe working procedures should assume that disturbance of the residue etc will release gas, fume or vapour (see paragraph 53).

- *Contamination*

  Contamination may arise from adjacent plant, processes, gas mains or surrounding land, soil or strata. Gases and liquids may leak or may have leaked into the confined space from adjacent plant, installations, processes or landfill sites. This is a particular risk where confined spaces are below ground because they can be contaminated by substances from installations many metres away. In certain situations, water in ground strata and/or gases may enter the confined space from the surrounding land, soil or strata. For example, acid groundwater acting on limestone can lead to dangerous accumulations of carbon dioxide. Also, methane can occur from a number of sources including the decay of organic matter and can be released from groundwater. Methane and other gases can leach into groundwater and be released at distances remote from the source. Sewers can be affected over long distances by water surges, for example following sudden heavy rainfall upstream of where work is being carried out.

- *Oxygen deficiency and oxygen enrichment*

  There are substantial risks if the concentration of oxygen in the atmosphere varies significantly from normal (ie 20.8%). For example, oxygen enrichment will increase flammability of clothing and other combustible materials. Conversely a relatively small reduction in the oxygen percentage can lead to impaired mental ability. The effects are very rapid and generally there will be no warning to alert the senses. This can happen even in circumstances where only a person's head is inside a confined space. Very low oxygen concentrations (ie below 16%) can lead to unconsciousness and death. Any difference in oxygen content from normal should be investigated, the risk assessed, and appropriate measures taken in the light of the risk.

- *Physical dimensions*

  You must consider the possible effects of the dimensions and layout of the confined space. Air quality can differ if the space contains remote or low-lying compartments. You should also take account of isolated pockets or regions within the space when choosing ventilation methods (see paragraphs 51 and 52).

(b) You should assess hazards that arise directly from the work to be undertaken in the confined space. The work itself may produce the hazard. Alternatively, conditions may become hazardous when work is done in conjunction with residues, contamination etc. Work being done on the exterior of the confined space (eg external welding) could also generate hazardous conditions within. Hazards that can be introduced into a space that may otherwise be safe include:

9

- *Cleaning chemicals*

  Chemicals that might be used for cleaning purposes could affect the atmosphere directly or interact with residual substances present in the confined space.

- *Sources of ignition*

  Welding could act as a source of ignition for flammable gases, vapours (eg from residues), dusts, plastics and many other materials which may burn leading to a fire or explosion. Welding on the outside of a confined space can easily ignite materials in contact with the metal on the inside. Tools and equipment, including lighting, may need to be inherently safe or specially protected where they are likely to be used in potentially flammable or explosive atmospheres so that they do not present a source of ignition.

(c) You should assess the need to isolate the confined space to prevent dangers arising from outside. For example:

- *Ingress of substances*

  There may be a risk of substances (liquids, gases, steam, water, raw materials) from nearby processes and services entering the confined space. This could be caused by the inadvertent operation of machinery. Consequently, you should normally disconnect power to such equipment and measures should be taken to ensure that it cannot be reconnected until it is safe to do so, taking care not to isolate vital services such as sprinkler systems, communications etc (inert gas flooding is dealt with at paragraph 87). Also, measures are needed to prevent the substance normally held in the confined space from being automatically delivered (see paragraphs 57 and 58). There may also be a risk of carbon monoxide, carbon dioxide and nitrogen dioxide present in the exhaust of combustion engines that could enter the confined space (see paragraphs 61 and 62).

(d) You should assess the requirements for emergency rescue arrangements. Possible emergencies should be anticipated and appropriate rescue arrangements made. The likely risks, and therefore the equipment and measures needed for a rescue by nearby employees need to be identified (see paragraphs 80-92). Further details about the role of the emergency services are dealt with in paragraph 91.

PREVENTING THE NEED FOR ENTRY

Confined Spaces Regulations 1997

Work in confined spaces

(1)   No person at work shall enter a confined space to carry out work for any purpose unless it is not reasonably practicable to achieve that purpose without such entry.

28 Employers have a duty to prevent employees, or others who are to any extent within the employer's control, such as contractors, from entering or working inside a confined space where it is reasonably practicable to undertake the work without entering the space. Similarly, the self-employed should not enter or work inside a confined space where it is reasonably practicable to undertake the work without entering it.

29 In every situation, the employer or the self-employed must consider what measures can be taken to enable the work to be carried out without the need to enter the confined space. The measures might involve modifying the confined space itself to avoid the need for entry, or to enable the work to be undertaken from outside the space. In many cases it will involve modifying working practices.

30 The following are examples of modified working practices preventing the need for entry:

● it is usually possible to test the atmosphere or sample the contents of confined spaces from outside using appropriate long tools and probes etc;

● in some cases you can clean a confined space, or remove residues from it, from the outside using water jetting, steam or chemical cleaning, long-handled tools, or in-place cleaning systems;

● blockages can be cleared in silos where grain or other solids can 'bridge' or where voids can form by the use of remotely-operated rotating flail devices, vibrators and air purgers which avoid the need to enter the space;

● in some cases it is possible to see what is happening inside without going in by looking in through a porthole, sightglass, grille or hole. If the sightglass tends to become blocked, it can be cleaned with a wiper and washer. Lighting can be provided inside or by shining in through a window. The use of closed circuit television systems (CCTV) may be appropriate in some cases.

Duties with regard to the design and construction of confined spaces

Health and Safety at Work etc Act 1974, section 6 (see Appendix 1)

Construction (Design and Management) Regulations 1994, regulation 13 (see Appendix 3 for details of guidance on regulations)

31 Section 6 of the Health and Safety at Work etc Act 1974 places a duty on designers, manufacturers, importers and suppliers of articles for use at work to ensure, so far as is reasonably practicable, that the article is so designed and constructed that it will be safe and without risk to health. Also, the Provision and Use of Work Equipment Regulations 1992 (regulation 5) places a duty on employers to ensure that work equipment is so constructed or adapted so that it will not affect the health or safety of any person when used or provided for the intended purpose.

32 Where plant and equipment unavoidably include confined spaces, designers, manufacturers, importers, suppliers, erectors and installers should eliminate or, where this is not possible, minimise the need to enter such spaces both during normal use or working, and for cleaning and maintenance.

33 Regulation 13 of the Construction (Design and Management) Regulations 1994 places a duty on designers to ensure that any design includes

adequate regard to the need to avoid foreseeable risks to the health and safety of any person on the structure at any time.

34   You can take a variety of measures to remove the need for people having to enter a confined space to work. However, there may be specific methods of working such as tunnelling, which although creating a confined space may nevertheless be the best overall option in view of the risk assessment. Engineers, architects, contractors and others who design, construct or modify buildings, structures etc, should aim to eliminate or minimise the need to enter a confined space. For example, conical bases on process vessels can be designed so that in-place cleaning systems can flush out debris effectively. Both normal working, cleaning, inspection, and maintenance work should be considered at the design stage. To ensure entirely new hazards are not introduced, designers will need to consult users carefully about their requirements. Where it is not reasonably practicable to avoid entry the design should incorporate easy access, taking account of requirements in the event of emergencies. For example, the design should incorporate manholes sited at the bottom or low down in the structure and the suitability of access and working platforms etc should be considered (see paragraphs 93-98). Design of the space itself should include provision of sample points, nozzles etc for atmospheric testing.

SAFE WORKING IN CONFINED SPACES

Confined Spaces Regulations 1997

Work in confined spaces

(2)   Without prejudice to paragraph (1) above, so far as is reasonably practicable, no person at work shall enter or carry out any work in or (other than as a result of an emergency) leave a confined space otherwise than in accordance with a system of work which, in relation to any relevant specified risks, renders that work safe and without risks to health.

35   **Where it is not reasonably practicable to avoid entering a confined space to undertake work, the employer or self-employed person is responsible for ensuring that a safe system of work is used. In designing a safe system of work, they should give priority to eliminating the source of any danger before deciding what precautions are needed for entry.**

Precautions to be included in the safe system of work

36   **The precautions required in a safe system of work will depend on the nature of the confined space and the risk assessment (see paragraphs 20-27). For example, the risks involved and precautions needed for cleaning car interiors with solvents will be relatively straightforward by comparison with those involved when undertaking welding work inside a chemical reactor vessel, or work in a sewer. The main elements to consider when designing a safe system of work, and which may form the basis of a 'permit-to-work' (see paragraphs 75-78), are:**

Supervision

37   The degree of supervision should be based on the findings of the risk assessment. In some cases an employer might simply instruct an employee how to do the work and then periodically check that all is well, for example, if the work is routine, the precautions straightforward, and all the arrangements for safety can be properly controlled by the person carrying out the work. It is more likely that the risk assessment will identify a level of risk that requires the appointment of a competent person (see paragraph 22(b)) to supervise the work and who may need to remain present while the work is being undertaken. It will be the supervisor's role to ensure that the permit-to-work system, where applicable, operates properly, the necessary safety precautions are taken, and that anyone in the vicinity of the confined space is informed of the work being done.

Competence for confined spaces working

38   To be competent to work safely in confined spaces, adequate training (see paragraph 113) and experience in the particular work involved is essential. Training standards must be appropriate to the task, and to the individual's roles and responsibilities, so that work can be carried out safely (see paragraph 79). Where the risk assessment indicates that properly trained individuals can work for periods without supervision, you will need to check that they are competent to follow the established safe system of work and have been provided with adequate information and instruction about the work to be done.

Communications

39   An adequate communication system will be needed and should enable communication:

- **between those inside the confined space;**

- **between those inside the confined space and those outside; and**

- **to summon help in case of emergency.**

Whatever system is used, and it can be based on speech, tugs on a rope, the telephone, radio etc, it is important that all messages can be communicated easily, rapidly and unambiguously between relevant people. Consider whether the communication methods are appropriate for any workers wearing breathing apparatus. The communication system should also cover the need for those outside the space to raise the alarm and set in motion emergency rescue procedures (see paragraph 80). Equipment such as telephones and radios should be specially protected so that they do not present a source of ignition where there is a risk of flammable or potentially explosive atmospheres.

Testing/monitoring the atmosphere

40   The atmosphere within a confined space may need testing for hazardous gas, fume or vapour or to check the concentration of oxygen prior to entry. Testing will be needed where knowledge of the confined space, for example, from information about its previous contents or chemicals used in a previous activity in the space, indicates that the atmosphere might be contaminated or to any extent unsafe to breathe, or where any doubt exists as to the condition of the atmosphere. It will also be needed where the atmosphere was known to be contaminated previously, was ventilated as a consequence, and needs to be tested to check the result.

41   Where the atmosphere in the space may not be safe to breathe and requires testing, the findings of the risk assessment may indicate that testing should be carried out on each occasion that the confined space is re-entered, even where the atmosphere initially was found to be safe to breathe. Regular monitoring of the atmosphere may also be necessary to check that there is no change in the atmosphere while the work is being carried out, particularly where there is a known possibility of adverse changes in the atmosphere during the work. The conditions should be continuously monitored when, for example, forced ventilation is being used, and where the work activity could give rise to changes in the atmosphere. The exact testing, retesting and monitoring requirements should be defined by a competent person (see paragraph 22(b)) within the safe system of work.

42   Local emergency services attending an emergency incident may necessarily require the immediate use of self-contained breathing apparatus, under controlled and monitored entry conditions, without following the testing procedures at paragraph 40. This is due to the constraints on effecting an immediate rescue. Further information on the role of the public emergency services is given in paragraph 91.

43   The choice of testing equipment will depend on the circumstances and knowledge of possible contaminants. For example, when testing for

toxic or asphyxiating atmospheres suitably calibrated chemical detector tubes or portable atmospheric monitoring equipment may be appropriate. However, in some cases equipment specifically designed to measure for flammable or explosive atmospheres will be required. All such equipment should be specially suited for use in these atmospheres. Testing equipment should also be in good working order and where necessary calibrated and checked in accordance with the intervals and recommendations accompanying the equipment, or at other suitable intervals. Explosimeters will need to be calibrated for different gases or vapours.

44   Testing to measure the oxygen content should be carried out before testing for concentration of flammable gases, followed by any further tests for toxic gases, vapours and dusts. Additional tests may be required for the presence of contaminants in liquid or solid form when the risk assessment indicates that they may be present. It is important not to overlook the flammable properties of substances that also have toxic properties, even if they are only slightly toxic.

45   Testing should be carried out by persons who are not only competent in the practice and aware of the existing standards for the relevant airborne contaminates being measured but are also instructed and trained in the risks involved. Those carrying out the testing should also be capable of interpreting the results and taking any necessary action. Records should be kept of the results and findings.

46   The atmosphere in a confined space can often be tested from the outside, without the need for entry, drawing samples through a long probe. Where flexible sample tubing is used, ensure that it is not impeded by kinks, blockages, blocked or restricted nozzles and that sufficient time is allowed for samples of the atmosphere to displace the normal air in the probe. It is important that the atmosphere in sufficiently representative samples of the space is tested to check for pockets of poor air quality, especially if there is any doubt about the thoroughness of ventilation. If it becomes necessary for the tester to enter the confined space, the work then should be carried out in accordance with the advice in this guidance.

Gas purging

47   Where the risk assessment has identified the presence or possible presence of flammable or toxic gases or vapours there may be a need to purge the gas or vapour from the confined space. This can be done with air or an inert gas where toxic contaminants are present, but with inert gas only where there are flammable contaminants. You can only use inert gas for purging flammable gas or vapour because any purging with air could produce a flammable mixture within the confined space. Where purging has been carried out, the atmosphere will need to be tested to check that purging has been effective, and that it is safe to breathe before allowing people to enter.

48   In circumstances where the safest method of removing a flammable or explosive hazard is by purging with inert gas, for instance using nitrogen displacement, and the work cannot be carried out from a safe position outside the confined space, you will need to put in place a permit-to-work system that identifies the standard of protection of all exposed persons. This would include use of full breathing apparatus.

49   Take account of the possibility of exposure both to employees and non-employees from vented gases as a result of purging. When carrying out purging, take precautions to protect those outside the confined space from toxic, flammable, irritating gases and vapours etc.

50   Good ventilation and a supply of breathable air are essential. Inhaling an atmosphere that contains no oxygen can cause loss of consciousness in a matter of seconds because such an atmosphere not only fails to provide oxygen but may also displace oxygen in the bloodstream. When the atmosphere inhaled contains some oxygen, the loss of oxygen from the bloodstream takes place more slowly. Nevertheless victims will feel very fatigued and will find it difficult to help themselves because of the irrationality induced by lack of oxygen. Prolonged exposure to such an atmosphere can result in loss of consciousness. The speed at which unconsciousness can result after exposure to an inert atmosphere is seldom appreciated and may have been a factor in some fatalities where rescue without proper breathing apparatus or respiratory protection has been attempted in such atmospheres.

Ventilation

51   Some confined spaces are enclosed to the extent that they require mechanical ventilation to provide sufficient fresh air to replace the oxygen that is being used up by people working in the space, and to dilute and remove gas, fume or vapour produced by the work. This can be done by using a blower fan and trunking and/or an exhaust fan or ejector and trunking (provided that there is an adequate supply of fresh air to replace the used air). Fresh air should be drawn from a point where it is not contaminated either by used air or other pollutants. Never introduce additional oxygen into a confined space to 'sweeten' the air as this can lead to oxygen enrichment in the atmosphere that can render certain substances (eg grease) liable to spontaneous combustion, and will greatly increase the combustibility of other materials. Oxygen above the normal concentration in air may also have a toxic effect if inhaled.

52   When considering the ventilation method, take account of the layout of the space, the position of openings etc and the properties of the pollutants, so that circulation of air for ventilation is effective. Natural ventilation may suffice if there is sufficient top and bottom openings in a vessel. For example, if a small tank containing heavy vapour has a single top manhole it may be sufficient to exhaust from the bottom of the tank with a ventilation duct whilst allowing 'make-up' air to enter through the manhole. For complicated spaces where several pockets of gas or vapour might collect, a more complex ventilation system will be needed to ensure thorough ventilation. Forced ventilation is normally preferable to exhaust ventilation (which has only a local benefit). It is essential to ensure that extract ventilation is routed away from possible sources of re-entry. In all cases it is important that an airline or trunking should be introduced at, or extend to, the bottom of the vessel to ensure removal of heavy gas or vapour and effective circulation of air.

Removal of residues

53   Cleaning or removal of residues is often the purpose of confined space work. In some cases residues will need to be removed to allow other work to be undertaken safely. Appropriate measures should be

taken where risks from the residues are identified. For example, dangerous substances (such as hazardous gas, fume or vapour) can be released when residues are disturbed or, particularly, when heat is applied to them. The measures might include the use of powered ventilation equipment, specially protected electrical equipment for use in hazardous atmospheres, respiratory protective equipment (see paragraphs 99 and 100) and atmospheric monitoring (see paragraph 40-46). The cleaning or removal process might need to be repeated to ensure that all residues have been removed, and in some cases might need to deal with residues trapped in sludge, scale or other deposits, brickwork, or behind loose linings, in liquid traps, joints in vessels, in pipe bends, or in other places where removal is difficult.

Isolation from gases, liquids, and other flowing materials

54   Confined spaces will often need to be isolated from ingress of substances that could pose a risk to those working within the space.

55   An effective method is to disconnect the confined space completely from every item of plant either removing a section of pipe or duct or by inserting blanks. If blanks are used, the spectacle type with one lens solid and the other a ring, makes checking easier. When disconnection in this way cannot be done one alternative is a suitable, reliable valve that is locked shut, providing there is no possibility of it allowing anything to pass through when locked, or of being unlocked when people are inside the confined space.

56   Barriers such as a single brick wall, a water seal, or shut-off valves or those sealed with sand or loam to separate one section of plant from another, are sometimes present at a confined space and offer some degree of isolation of the space. However, these barriers are usually provided for normal working and may not provide the level of safety protection necessary for the high risks often found in confined spaces. A more substantial means of isolation may therefore be needed. Whatever means of isolation is used it needs to be tested to ensure it is sufficiently reliable by checking for substances to see if isolation has been effective.

Isolation from mechanical and electrical equipment

57   Some confined spaces contain electrical and mechanical equipment with power supplied from outside the space. Unless the risk assessment specifically enables the system of work to allow power to remain on, either for the purposes of the task being undertaken or as vital services (ie lighting, vital communications, fire-fighting, pumping where flooding is a risk, or cables distributing power to other areas) the power should be disconnected, separated from the equipment, and a check made to ensure isolation has been effective. This could include locking off the switch and formally securing the key in accordance with a permit-to-work, until it is no longer necessary to control access. Lock and tag systems can be useful here, where each operator has their own lock and key giving self-assurance of the inactivated mechanism or system. Check there is no stored energy of any kind left in the system that could activate the equipment inadvertently.

Selection and use of suitable equipment

58   Any equipment provided for use in a confined space needs to be suitable for the purpose. Where there is a risk of a flammable gas seeping into a confined space and which could be ignited by electrical sources (eg a portable hand lamp), specially protected electrical

equipment needs to be used, for example, a lamp certified for use in explosive atmospheres. Note that specially designed low voltage portable lights, while offering protection against electrocution, could nevertheless still present ignition sources and are not in themselves safer in flammable or potentially explosive atmospheres. All equipment should be carefully selected bearing in mind the conditions and risks where it will be used. Earthing should be considered to prevent static charge build-up. In addition to isolation (see paragraph 57), mechanical equipment may need to be secured against free rotation, as people may tread or lean on it, and risk trapping or falling. Further details on requirements for certain other equipment, including requirements for examination and maintenance, are dealt with in paragraphs 103-112.

Personal protective equipment and respiratory protective equipment

59   So far as is reasonably practicable you should ensure that a confined space is safe to work in without the need for personal protective equipment (PPE) and respiratory protective equipment (RPE) which should be a last resort, except for rescue work (including the work of the emergency services). Use of PPE and RPE may be identified as necessary in your risk assessment, in which case it needs to be suitable and should be provided and used by those entering and working in confined spaces. Such equipment is in addition to engineering controls and safe systems of work. The type of PPE provided will depend on the hazards identified but, for example, might include safety lines and harnesses, and suitable breathing apparatus. Take account of foreseeable hazards that might arise, and the need for emergency evacuation (see also paragraphs 99-102).

60   Wearing respiratory protective equipment and personal protective equipment can contribute to heat stress. In extreme situations cooling air may be required for protective suits. Footwear and clothing may also require insulating properties, for example, to prevent softening of plastics that could lead to distortion of components such as visors, airhoses and crimped connections. See paragraphs 100 and 83 for details of when 'escape breathing apparatus' (or self-rescuers) are appropriate.

Portable gas cylinders and internal combustion engines

61   Never use petrol-fuelled internal combustion engines in confined spaces. Gas cylinders should not normally be used within a confined space unless special precautions are taken. Portable gas cylinders for heat, power or light, and diesel-fuelled internal combustion engines are nearly as dangerous as petrol-fuelled engines, and are inappropriate unless exceptional precautions are taken. Where their use cannot be avoided, adequate ventilation needs to be provided to prevent a build-up of harmful gas, and to allow internal combustion engines to operate properly. The exhaust from engines should be vented to a safe place well away from the confined space, downwind of any ventilator intakes for the confined space, and the means checked for leakage within the confined space. In tunnelling, normal practice is to provide a high level of ventilation and additional precautions to minimise emissions. Fuelling of portable engine-driven equipment should be conducted outside the confined space except in rare cases where it is not reasonably practicable, such as in some tunnelling work. Using such equipment within the space requires constant atmospheric monitoring of the space.

62 Check gas equipment and gas pipelines for gas leaks before entry into the confined space. At the end of every work period remove gas cylinders, including those forming welding sets, from the confined space in case a slow leak contaminates the atmosphere within the space.

Gas supplied by pipes and hoses

63 The use of pipes and hoses for conveying oxygen or flammable gases into a confined space should be controlled to minimise the risks. It is important that at the end of every working period, other than during short interruptions, the supply valves for pipes and hoses are securely closed before the pipes and hoses are withdrawn from the confined space to a place that is well ventilated. Where pipes and hoses cannot be removed, they should be disconnected from the gas supply at a point outside the confined space and their contents safely vented.

Access and egress

64 You should provide a safe way in and out of the confined space. Wherever possible allow quick, unobstructed and ready access. The means of escape must be suitable for use by the individual who enters the confined space so that they can quickly escape in an emergency. Suitable means to prevent access should be in place when there is no need for anybody to work in the confined space. The safe system of work should ensure that everyone has left the confined space during 'boxing-up' operations particularly when the space is complicated and extensive, for example in boilers, cableways and culverts where there can be numerous entry/exit points.

65 The size of openings to confined spaces needs to be adequate. Openings affording safe access to confined spaces, and through divisions, partitions or obstructions within such spaces, need to be sufficiently large and free from obstruction to allow the passage of persons wearing the necessary protective clothing and equipment, and to allow adequate access for rescue purposes. Guidance on the dimensions for manhole openings can be found in paragraphs 93-98.

66 There should be a safety sign that is clear and conspicuous to prohibit unauthorised entry alongside openings that allow for safe access.

Fire prevention

67 Wherever possible flammable and combustible materials should not be stored in confined spaces that have not been specifically created or allocated for that purpose. If they accumulate as a result of work they should be removed as soon as possible and before they begin to create a risk. Where flammable materials need to be located in a confined space the quantity of the material should be kept to a minimum. In most cases flammable materials should not be stored in confined spaces; however there may be special cases where this is necessary for example, in tunnelling. In these cases they should be stored in suitable fire-resistant containers. If there is a risk of flammable or potentially explosive atmospheres, take precautions to eliminate the risk such as removal by cleaning, effective use of thorough ventilation, and control of the sources of ignition.

Lighting

68   Adequate and suitable lighting, including emergency lighting, should be provided. For example, the lighting will need to be specially protected if used where flammable or potentially explosive atmospheres are likely to occur. Other gases may be present that could break down thermally on the unprotected hot surfaces of a lighting system and produce other toxic products. Lighting may need to be protected against knocks (eg by a wire cage), and/or be waterproof. Where water is present in the space, suitable plug/socket connectors capable of withstanding wet or damp conditions should be used and protected by residual current devices (RCDs) suitable for protection against electric shock. The position of lighting may also be important, for example to give ample clearance for work or rescue to be carried out unobstructed.

Static electricity

69   Exclude static discharges, and all sources of ignition if there is a risk of a flammable or explosive atmosphere in the confined space. All conducting items such as steel trunking and airlines should be bonded and effectively earthed. If cleaning operations are to be carried out assess the risks posed by the use or presence of high resistivity materials (such as synthetic plastics) in and adjacent to the confined space.

70   Some equipment is prone to static build-up due to its insulating characteristics, for example, most plastics. There is also a high risk of electrostatic discharge from some equipment used for steam or water jetting. Static discharges can also arise from clothing containing cotton or wool. Consider selecting safer alternative equipment and antistatic footwear and clothing.

Smoking

71   Smoking should be prohibited in confined spaces. The results of the risk assessment may indicate that it would be necessary to extend the exclusion area to a distance beyond the confined space, for example, 5-10 m.

Emergencies and rescue

72   The arrangements for the rescue of persons in the event of an emergency, required under regulation 5 of the Confined Spaces Regulations, need to be suitable and sufficient and, where appropriate, there will also be a need for the necessary equipment to enable resuscitation procedures to be carried out. The arrangements should be in place before any person enters or works in a confined space (see paragraphs 80-92).

Limiting working time

73   There may be a need to limit the time period that individuals are allowed to work in a confined space. This may be appropriate where, for example, respiratory protective equipment is used, or under extreme conditions of temperature and humidity; or the confined space is so small that movement is severely restricted. For a large confined space and multiple entries, a logging or tally system may be necessary to check everyone in and out and to control duration of entry.

74   To be effective a safe system of work needs to be in writing. A safe system of work sets out the work to be done and the precautions to be taken. When written down it is a formal record that all foreseeable hazards and risks have been considered in advance. The safe procedure consists of all appropriate precautions taken in the correct sequence. In practice a safe system of work will only ever be as good as its implementation.

Use of a permit-to-work procedure

75   A permit-to-work system is a formal written system and is usually required where there is a reasonably foreseeable risk of serious injury in entering or working in the confined space. The permit-to-work procedure is an extension of the safe system to work, not a replacement for it. The use of a permit-to-work system does not, by itself, make the job safe. It supports the safe system, providing a ready means of recording findings and authorisations required to proceed with the entry. It also contains information, for example, time limits on entry, results of the gas testing, and other information that may be required during an emergency and which, when the job is completed, can also provide historical information on original entry conditions. A permit-to-work system is appropriate, for example:

(a)   to ensure that the people working in the confined space are aware of the hazards involved and the identity, nature and extent of the work to be carried out;

(b)   to ensure there is a formal check undertaken confirming elements of a safe system of work are in place. This needs to take place before people are allowed to enter or work in the confined space;

(c)   where there is a need to coordinate or exclude, using controlled and formal procedures, other people and their activities where they could affect work or conditions in the confined space;

(d)   if the work requires the authorisation of more than one person, or there is a time-limit on entry. It may also be needed if communications with the outside are other than by direct speech, or if particular respiratory protective and/or personal protective equipment is required.

A permit-to-work should be cancelled once the operations to which it applies have finished.

76   The nature of permit-to-work procedures will vary in their scope depending on the job, and the risks. A permit-to-work system is unlikely to be needed where, for example:

(a)   the assessed risks are low and can be controlled easily; and

(b)   the system of work is very simple; and

(c)   you know that other work activities being carried out cannot affect safe working in the confined space.

If an assessed risk is subsequently eliminated entirely, and there is no foreseeable chance of it recurring, you can consider giving unrestricted entry provided the above conditions apply.

21

77   The decision not to adopt a permit-to-work system should be taken by a competent person (see paragraph 22(b)), where necessary following consultation with specialists, and bearing in mind the findings of the risk assessment (see paragraphs 20-27) and the need to ensure a safe system of work (see paragraphs 35-74).

78   Useful information relating to the general preparation and application of permits-to-work can be found in the Oil Industry Advisory Committee guidance booklet *Permit to work systems in the petroleum industry* (see Appendix 3).

Suitability for work in confined spaces

79   **The competent person carrying out the risk assessment (see paragraph 22(b)) for work in confined spaces will need to consider the suitability of individuals in view of the particular work to be done (see paragraph 38). Where the risk assessment highlights exceptional constraints from the physical layout, the competent person may need to check that individuals are of suitable build. This may be necessary to protect both the individual and others who could be affected by the work to be done. The competent person may need to consider other factors about an individual, for example, concerning claustrophobia or fitness to wear breathing apparatus, and medical advice on an individual's suitability for the work may be needed.**

EMERGENCY PROCEDURES

Confined Spaces Regulations 1997

Emergency arrangements

(1)   Without prejudice to regulation 4 of these Regulations, no person at work shall enter or carry out work in a confined space unless there have been prepared in respect of that confined space suitable and sufficient arrangements for the rescue of persons in the event of an emergency, whether or not arising out of a specified risk.

(2)   Without prejudice to the generality of paragraph (1) above, the arrangements referred to in that paragraph shall not be suitable and sufficient unless -

(a)   they reduce, so far as is reasonably practicable, the risks to the health and safety of any person required to put the arrangements for rescue into operation; and

(b)   they require, where the need for resuscitation of any person is a likely consequence of a relevant specified risk, the provision and maintenance of such equipment as is necessary to enable resuscitation procedures to be carried out.

(3)   Whenever there arises any circumstance to which the arrangements referred to in paragraph (1) above relate, those arrangements, or the relevant part or parts of those arrangements, shall immediately be put into operation.

80   **Arrangements for emergency rescue will depend on the nature of the confined space, the risks identified and the likely nature of an emergency rescue. Account needs to be taken not only of accidents arising from a specified risk, but also any other accident in which a person needs to be recovered from a confined space, for example,**

incapacitation following a fall. To be suitable and sufficient the arrangements for rescue and resuscitation should include consideration of:

	Paragraph
Rescue and resuscitation equipment	81-84
Raising the alarm and rescue	85
Safeguarding the rescuers	86
Fire safety	87-88
Control of plant	89
First aid	90
Public emergency services	91
Training	92

Rescue and resuscitation equipment

81   Rescue equipment provided should be appropriate in view of the likely emergencies identified in the risk assessment, and should be properly maintained. If resuscitation has been identified as a likely consequence, provision will need to be made for appropriate training to enable resuscitation procedures to be carried out (see paragraph 92), and this may include use of appropriate resuscitation equipment (see paragraph 84). In determining if resuscitation is likely to be needed, consideration should be given to experience gained from knowledge of previous incidents.

82   Rescue equipment will often include lifelines and lifting equipment (since even the strongest person is unlikely to be able to lift or handle an unconscious person on their own using only a rope), additional sets of breathing apparatus (see paragraph 99) and first aid equipment.

83   'Self-rescue ' equipment (see paragraph 100), may be appropriate for use in situations where there will be time to react to an anticipated emergency situation, for example, smoke logging in tunnels or reacting to atmospheric monitoring devices. They should be made available only where the type provided is suitable for the hazard expected in the emergency situation. They are not a substitute for respiratory protective equipment (see paragraph 99).

84   Resuscitation procedures include respiratory and circulatory resuscitation procedures. These are simple procedures that most people would be capable of carrying out provided they have been trained. Training and refresher training are essential since the speed with which resuscitation is started is often as important as how well it is done. Ancillary equipment may be needed for oral resuscitation: these avoid direct contact between the mouths of the victim and rescuer, for example, by using special tubes and mouthpieces. However, if resuscitation is needed as a result of exposure to toxic gases, oral methods are not appropriate since they could put the rescuer at risk. In some cases equipment for artificial respiration as a follow-up to, or in place of, oral resuscitation is appropriate. This equipment should only be operated by someone with the necessary specialist training, or it can be kept available, properly maintained, on site for use by a person providing professional medical help.

23

Raising the alarm and rescue

85   There should be measures to enable those in the confined space to communicate to others outside the space who can initiate rescue procedures or summon help in an emergency. The emergency can be communicated in a number of ways, for example by the tug of a rope, by radio or by means of a 'lone worker' alarm. Whatever the system it should be reliable and tested frequently. Exceptionally, if justified on grounds of risk or from knowledge of previous incidents involving similar work, one or more people dedicated to the rescue role, and outside the confined space will be required to keep those inside in constant direct visual sight in case of emergency.

Safeguarding the rescuers

86   Multiple fatalities have occurred when rescuers have been overcome by the same conditions that have affected the people they have tried to rescue. To prevent this, it is essential that those who have been assigned a rescue role, for example, members of an in-house or works rescue team (see paragraph 92) are themselves protected against the cause of the emergency. The precautions necessary to protect the rescuers should be considered during the risk assessment, and adequate provisions made when preparing suitable and sufficient emergency arrangements.

Fire safety

87   Advice on fire safety precautions and measures may be obtained from the local fire service. Inert gas flooding of the confined space must not take place when people are within the space.

88   Where there is a risk of fire, appropriate fire extinguishers may need to be kept in the confined space at the entry point. In some situations, a sprinkler system may be appropriate. In the event of a fire, the local fire service should be called in case the fire cannot be contained or extinguished. Care is needed when deciding whether or not the ventilation system should be kept working or switched off because either course may affect the chances of escape or rescue. Continued use of the ventilation system may also affect the development of the fire, because forced air may fan the flames.

Control of plant

89   There may be a need to shut down adjacent or nearby plant before attempting an emergency rescue, either because the plant could be the cause of the emergency or safe entry cannot be gained without the plant being shut down.

First aid

90   Appropriate first aid equipment should be provided and available for emergencies and provide first aid until professional medical help arrives. First aiders should be trained to deal with the foreseeable injuries.

Public emergency services

91   In some circumstances, for example where there are prolonged operations in confined spaces and the risks justify it, there may be advantage in prior notification to the local emergency services (eg local Fire or Ambulance Service) before the work is undertaken. If such notification is thought

necessary, the emergency services should be consulted and confirmation obtained about the information they would find useful. In all cases, however, arrangements must be in place for the rapid notification of the emergency services should an accident occur. On arrival, the emergency services should be given all known information about the conditions and risks of entering and/or leaving the confined space before entering it to attempt a rescue. This information is then available at the scene of an incident where a necessarily dynamic risk assessment by the local emergency services can be undertaken.

Training

92   Those likely to be involved in any emergency rescue should be trained for that purpose. The training needs for each individual will vary according to their designated role. It is important that refresher training is organised and available on a regular basis, for example annually. Training should include the following, where appropriate:

(a)   the likely causes of an emergency;

(b)   use of rescue equipment, eg breathing apparatus, lifelines, and where necessary a knowledge of its construction and working;

(c)   the check procedures to be followed when donning and using apparatus;

(d)   checking of correct functioning and/or testing of emergency equipment (for immediate use and to enable specific periodic maintenance checks);

(e)   identifying defects and dealing with malfunctions and failures of equipment during use;

(f)   works, site or other local emergency procedures including the initiation of an emergency response;

(g)   instruction on how to shut down relevant process plant as appropriate (this knowledge would be required by anyone likely to perform a rescue);

(h)   resuscitation procedures and, where appropriate, the correct use of relevant ancillary equipment and any resuscitation equipment provided (if intended to be operated by those receiving emergency rescue training);

(i)   emergency first aid and the use of the first aid equipment provided;

(j)   use of fire-fighting equipment;

(k)   liaison with local emergency services in the event of an incident, providing relevant information about conditions and risks, and providing appropriate space and facilities to enable the emergency services to carry out their tasks; and

(l)   rescue techniques including regular and periodic rehearsals/exercises. This could include the use of a full-weight dummy. Training should be realistic and not just drill based, and should relate to practice and familiarity with equipment.

Further details on training are covered in paragraphs 113-116.

PLANT AND EQUIPMENT

Legal duties in respect of plant and equipment for use in confined spaces are set out in Appendix 1, which is part of this Code

Size of openings to enable safe access to and egress from confined spaces

93   Experience has shown that the minimum size of an opening to allow access with full rescue facilities including self-contained breathing apparatus is 575 mm diameter. This size should normally be used for new plant, although the openings for some confined spaces may need to be larger depending on the circumstances, for example, to take account of a fully equipped employee, or the nature of the opening.

94   Existing plant may have narrower openings. It will therefore be necessary to check that a person wearing suitable equipment can safely and readily pass through such openings. Choice of airline breathing apparatus in such cases offers a more compact alternative to bulkier self-contained apparatus. Examples of plant where there are narrower openings include rail tank wagons and tank containers where an opening of 500 mm diameter is common, and in road tankers where the recognised size is 410 mm. Even smaller openings can be found in the highly specialised nature of access to certain parts of aircraft, such as to fuel tanks in wings. Precautions need to take account of such special cases.

95   The size and number of access and egress points should be assessed individually dependent upon the activities being carried out and the number of people involved. Large-scale evacuations may need larger routes and openings to prevent them becoming bottlenecks. Top openings to vessels, tanks etc should be avoided due to difficulty of access and rescue. Bottom or low manholes are preferable and may need access platforms. There may be occasions when access and egress is so tortuous, for example, in the double bottom of a ship, that temporary openings may be needed.

96   Different criteria apply when the critical entry dimensions extend over a significant length or height, as in the case of sewers, pipes, culverts, small tunnels and shafts. For example, it is recommended that people should not normally enter sewers of dimensions smaller than 0.9 m high by 0.6 m wide. Even this 'minimum size' may in certain circumstances be too small for reliance on a safe system of work alone. Additional measures may be needed, for example if there is a long distance between access points or the siting of the sewer invert, structural alterations to improve access may be appropriate. In the case of a shaft containing a ladder or step irons, 900 mm clear space is recommended between the ladder/steps and the back of the shaft. The spacing of manholes on sewers, or in the case of large gas mains etc, the absence of such access over considerable lengths may affect both the degree of natural ventilation and the ease with which people can be rescued.

97   Further guidance on appropriate recognised standards relevant to manholes and other confined spaces is contained in Appendix 2.

98   Practice drills including emergency rescues will help to check that the size of openings and entry procedures are satisfactory.

Respiratory protective equipment

99   Where respiratory protective equipment (RPE) is provided or used in connection with confined space entry or for emergency or

rescue, it should be suitable for the purpose for which it is intended, ie correctly selected and matched both to the job and the wearer. RPE will not normally be suitable unless it is breathing apparatus. For most cases breathing apparatus would provide the standard of protection for entry into confined spaces. Any RPE should comply with the Personal Protective Equipment (EC Directive) Regulations 1992 (displaying a 'CE mark'), or, where these provisions are not appropriate, be of a standard or to a type approved by HSE.

Guidance

100   Where the intention is to provide emergency breathing apparatus to ensure safe egress or escape, or for self-rescue in case of emergency, the type commonly called an 'escape breathing apparatus' or 'self-rescuer' (escape set) may be suitable. These types are intended to allow the user time to exit the hazard area. They are generally carried by the user or stationed inside the confined space, but are not used until needed. This equipment usually has a breathable supply of only short duration and provides limited protection to allow the user to move to a place of safety or refuge. This type of equipment is not suitable for normal work. Examples of emergency breathing apparatus or self-rescuers include:

(a)   the rebreathable type which consists of a tube and mouthpiece;

(b)   the 'escape set' which consists of a cylinder-fed positive pressure face mask or hood.

101   RPE of the canister respirator or cartridge type is not appropriate for entry into or work in most confined spaces. However, this type of equipment may have a role if account is taken of its limitations and where the risk is of exposure to low concentrations of hazardous contaminants. Such equipment does not protect against the risk of being overcome - for example, it does not provide adequate protection against high concentrations of gases and vapours - and should never be used in oxygen-deficient atmospheres. Canister or cartridge respirators also have a limited duration, in some cases about 15 minutes, which should be checked against the equipment supplier's recommendations. It is also important to check that they are still within their useable shelf-life.

102   In some circumstances entry without the continuous wearing of breathing apparatus may be possible. Several conditions must be satisfied to allow work in confined spaces without respiratory protective equipment:

●   a risk assessment must be done and a safe system of work in place including all required controls, for example, thorough and continuous general ventilation;

●   any airborne contamination must be of a generally non-toxic nature, or present in very low concentrations well below the relevant occupational exposure limits;

●   the level of oxygen needs to be adequate (see paragraph 27(a) on oxygen deficiency and oxygen enrichment).

ACOP

Other equipment

103   Ropes, harnesses, fall arrest gear, lifelines, first aid equipment, protective clothing and other special equipment provided or used for, or in connection with, confined space entry or, in case of emergency rescue or resuscitation, should be suitable for the purposes for which they are intended, and account taken of appropriate recognised standards where these exist.

104   When a safety harness and line are used, it is essential that the free end of the line is secured so that it can be used as part of the rescue procedure. In most cases the line should be secured outside the entry to the confined space. The harness and line should be adjusted and worn so that the wearer can be safely drawn through any manhole or opening. Lifting equipment may be necessary for this purpose. An appropriate harness fitted to the line should be of suitable construction, and made of suitable material to recognised standards capable of withstanding both the strain likely to be imposed, and attack from chemicals.

Maintenance of equipment

105   All equipment provided or used for the purposes of securing the health and safety of people in connection with confined space entry or for emergency or rescue, should be maintained in an efficient state, in efficient working order and in good repair. This should include periodic examination and testing as necessary. Some types of equipment, for example breathing apparatus, should be inspected each time before use.

106   The manufacturer or supplier's instructions will often provide advice on the frequency and type of examination.

Examination of equipment

107   The examination of RPE and resuscitating apparatus normally will comprise a thorough visual examination of all parts of the respirator, breathing or resuscitating apparatus, looking particularly at the integrity of the straps, facepieces, filters and valves. Any defects discovered by the examination, and which would undermine safe operation, should be remedied before further use.

108   The examination of ropes, harnesses, lifelines, protective clothing, and other special equipment normally will consist of a thorough visual examination of all their parts for deterioration or damage, in particular of those parts that are load-bearing. Examinations should be carried out regularly. In the case of protective clothing that is used only occasionally or where the conditions of use are unlikely to damage it, the interval between examinations may be greater.

109   Atmospheric monitoring equipment and special ventilating or other equipment provided or used in connection with confined space entry needs to be properly maintained. It should be examined thoroughly, and where necessary calibrated and checked in accordance with the intervals and recommendations accompanying the equipment or, if these are not specified, at such intervals considered suitable. The manufacturer's instructions, where they are available, are also relevant. Keep reports of all thorough examinations and records of calibration.

Test certificates and examination records

110   Properly supplied equipment used for lifting, such as ropes, harnesses, lifelines, rings, shackles, carabiners etc will have a certificate of test and safe working load when purchased. It is important to ensure they are not further tested (as this could weaken them). If they become damaged, they should be scrapped. Failing that, they should be returned to the manufacturer or other competent repairer who can carry out the necessary remedial work and supply a new certificate of test and safe working load for the repaired equipment.

111   The record of each thorough examination and test of equipment will normally include:

(a) the name and address of the employer or other person responsible for the equipment;

(b) particulars of the equipment and of the distinguishing number or mark, together with a description sufficient to identify it, and the name of the maker;

(c) the date of the examination and the name and signature of the person carrying out the examination and test;

(d) the condition of the equipment and particulars of any defect found;

(e) in the case of RPE and resuscitating apparatus incorporating compressed gas cylinders or electric motors, tests of the condition and efficiency of those parts, including tests of the pressure of oxygen or air in the supply cylinder;

(f) in the case of airline-fed RPE, the volume, flow and quality of the air. Where this is supplied from a mobile compressor the test should normally be made immediately before the first use of RPE in any new location;

(g) a brief description of any remedial action taken.

112 Records of the examination and tests of equipment should normally be kept for at least 5 years. The records may be in any suitable format and may consist of a suitable summary of the reports. Records need to be kept readily available for inspection by the employees, their representatives, or by inspectors appointed by the relevant enforcing authority or by employment medical advisers.

TRAINING

Health and Safety at Work etc Act 1974, section 2(2)(c)

(see Appendix 1)

113 Employers are required to provide such information, instruction, training and supervision as is necessary to ensure the health and safety at work of employees. Specific training for work in confined spaces will depend on an individual's previous experience and the type of work they will be doing. It is likely that this training will need to cover:

(a) an awareness of the Confined Spaces Regulations and in particular the need to avoid entry to a confined space, unless it is not reasonably practicable to do so, in accordance with regulation 4(1);

(b) an understanding of the work to be undertaken, the hazards, and the necessary precautions;

(c) an understanding of safe systems of work, with particular reference to 'permits-to-work' where appropriate;

(d) how emergencies arise, the need to follow prepared emergency arrangements (see paragraph 80), and the dangers of not doing so.

114 Training should also take into account the practical use of safety features and equipment, the identification of defects and, where appropriate, it should

29

involve demonstrations and practical exercises. It is important that trainees are familiar with both equipment and procedures before working for the first time in confined spaces.

115   Practical refresher training should be organised and available. The frequency with which refresher training is provided will depend upon how long since the type of work was last done, or if there have been changes to methods of work, safety procedures or equipment.

116   Training in specific safety features may include any or all of the following:

(a)   use of atmospheric testing equipment, and the action to take depending on the readings;

(b)   use of breathing apparatus and escape sets (self-rescuers), their maintenance, cleaning and storage;

(c)   use of other items of personal protective equipment;

(d)   instruction in the communication methods to be used whilst in the confined space.

Training in emergency rescue procedures is covered in paragraph 92.

Confined Spaces Regulations 1997

Regulation 6

Exemption certificates

(1)   Subject to paragraph (2) below, the Health and Safety Executive may, by a certificate in writing, exempt -

(a)   any person or class of persons; or

(b)   any type or class of confined space,

from the application of any of the requirements or prohibitions imposed by these Regulations, and any such exemption may be granted subject to conditions and to a limit of time and may be revoked at any time by the said Executive by a further certificate in writing.

(2)   The Executive shall not grant any such exemption unless, having regard to the circumstances of the case, and in particular to -

(a)   the conditions, if any, which it proposes to attach to the exemption; and

(b)   any other requirements imposed by or under any enactments which apply to the case,

it is satisfied that the health and safety of persons who are likely to be affected by the exemption will not be prejudiced in consequence of it.

Regulation 7

Defence in proceedings

(1)   In any proceedings for an offence for a contravention of regulation 5(3) of these Regulations it shall be a defence for that person charged to prove -

(a)   that the contravention was due to the act or default of another person not being one of his employees (hereinafter called "the other person"); and

(b)   that he took all reasonable precautions and exercised all due diligence to avoid the contravention.

(2)   The person charged shall not, without leave of the court, be entitled to rely on the defence referred to in paragraph (1) above unless, within a period ending seven clear days -

(a)   before the hearing to determine mode of trial, where the proceedings are in England or Wales; or

(b)   before the trial, where the proceedings are in Scotland,

he has served on the prosecutor a notice in writing giving such information identifying or assisting in the identification of the other person as was then in his possession.

(3)   Where a contravention of the provision referred to in paragraph (1) above by any person is due to the act or default of some other person, that other person shall be guilty of the offence which would, but for any defence under this regulation available to the first-mentioned person, be constituted by the act or default.

Repeal and revocations

(1)   Section 30 of the Factories Act 1961[a] is hereby repealed.

(2)   The instruments set out in column 1 of the Schedule to these Regulations are hereby revoked to the extent shown in column 3 of the said Schedule.

(a)   1961 c.34; section 30 was amended by SI 1983/978.

Revocation

Regulation 9

(1) *Instrument revoked*	(2) *Reference*	(3) *Extent of revocation*
Shipbuilding and Ship-repairing Regulations 1960	SI 1960/1932; relevant amending instruments are SI 1989/635 and SI 1992/2966	Regulations 48 to 52 and 54
The Shipbuilding (Reports on Breathing Apparatus, etc.) Order 1961	SI 1961/114	The whole Order
The Breathing Apparatus, etc. (Report on Examination) Order 1961	SI 1961/1345	The whole Order
The Agriculture (Poisonous Substances) Act 1952 (Repeals and Modifications) Regulations 1975	SI 1975/45	The whole Regulations
The Kiers Regulations 1938 (Metrication) Regulations 1981	SI 1981/1152	The whole Regulations
The Docks Regulations 1988	SI 1988/1655	Regulation 18

Relevant general health and safety law

Management of Health and Safety at Work Regulations 1992

Risk assessment

(1) Every employer shall make a suitable and sufficient assessment of -

(a) the risks to the health and safety of his employees to which they are exposed whilst they are at work; and

(b) the risks to the health and safety of persons not in his employment arising out of or in connection with the conduct by him of his undertaking,

for the purpose of identifying the measures he needs to take to comply with the requirements and prohibitions imposed upon him by or under the relevant statutory provisions.

(2) Every self-employed person shall make a suitable and sufficient assessment of -

(a) the risks to his own health and safety to which he is exposed whilst he is at work; and

(b) the risks to the health and safety of persons not in his employment arising out of or in connection with the conduct by him of his undertaking,

for the purpose of identifying the measures he needs to take to comply with the requirements and prohibitions imposed upon him by or under the relevant statutory provisions.

(3) Any assessment such as is referred to in paragraph (1) or (2) shall be reviewed by the employer or self-employed person who made it if -

(a) there is reason to suspect that it is no longer valid; or

(b) there has been a significant change in the matters to which it relates;

and where as a result of any such review changes to an assessment are required, the employer or self-employed person concerned shall make them.

(4) Where the employer employs five or more employees, he shall record -

(a) the significant findings of the assessment; and

(b) any group of his employees identified by it as being especially at risk.

Health and safety assistance

(1) Every employer shall, subject to paragraphs (6) and (7), appoint one or more competent persons to assist him in undertaking the measures he needs to take to comply with the requirements and prohibitions imposed upon him by or under the relevant statutory provisions.

(2)   Where an employer appoints persons in accordance with paragraph (1), he shall make arrangements for ensuring adequate co-operation between them.

(3)   The employer shall ensure that the number of persons appointed under paragraph (1), the time available for them to fulfil their functions and the means at their disposal are adequate having regard to the size of his undertaking, the risks to which his employees are exposed and the distribution of those risks throughout the undertaking.

(4)   The employer shall ensure that -

(a)   any person appointed by him in accordance with paragraph (1) who is not in his employment -

(i)   is informed of the factors known by him to affect, or suspected by him of affecting, the health and safety of any other person who may be affected by the conduct of his undertaking, and

(ii)   has access to the information referred to in regulation 8; and

(b)   any person appointed by him in accordance with paragraph (1) is given such information about any person working in his undertaking who is -

(i)   employed by him under a fixed-term contract of employment, or

(ii)   employed in an employment business,

as is necessary to enable that person properly to carry out the function specified in that paragraph.

(5)   A person shall be regarded as competent for the purposes of paragraph (1) where he has sufficient training and experience or knowledge and other qualities to enable him properly to assist in undertaking the measures referred to in that paragraph.

(6)   Paragraph (1) shall not apply to a self-employed employer who is not in partnership with any other person where he has sufficient training and experience or knowledge and other qualities properly to undertake the measures referred to in that paragraph himself.

(7)   Paragraph (1) shall not apply to individuals who are employers and who are together carrying on business in partnership where at least one of the individuals concerned has sufficient training and experience or knowledge and other qualities -

(a)   properly to undertake the measures he needs to take to comply with the requirements and prohibitions imposed upon him by or under the relevant statutory provisions; and

(b)   properly to assist his fellow partners in undertaking the measures they need to take to comply with the requirements and prohibitions imposed upon them by or under the relevant statutory provisions.

Section 2

Act

General duties of employers to their employees

(1)   It shall be the duty of every employer to ensure, so far as is reasonably practicable, the health, safety and welfare at work of all his employees.

(2)   Without prejudice to the generality of an employer's duty under the preceding subsection, the matters to which that duty extends include in particular -

(c)   the provision of such information, instruction, training and supervision as is necessary to ensure, so far as is reasonably practicable, the health and safety at work of his employees.

Section 6

Act

General duties of manufacturers etc as regards articles and substances for use at work

(1)   It shall be the duty of any person who designs, manufactures, imports or supplies any article for use at work -

(a)   to ensure, so far as is reasonably practicable, that the article is designed and constructed that it will be safe and without risks to health at all times when it is being set, used, cleaned or maintained by a person at work;

(b)   to carry out or arrange for the carrying out of such testing and examination as may be necessary for the performance of the duty imposed on him by the preceding paragraph;

(c)   to take such steps as are necessary to secure that persons supplied by that person with the article are provided with adequate information about the use for which the article is designed or has been tested and about any conditions necessary to ensure that it will be safe and without risks to health at all such times as are mentioned in paragraph (a) above and when it is being dismantled or disposed of; and

(d)   to take such steps as are necessary to secure, so far as is reasonably practicable, that persons so supplied are provided with all such revisions of information provided to them by virtue of the preceding paragraph as are necessary by reason of its becoming known that anything gives rise to a serious risk to health or safety.

Regulation 4

Regulation

Provision of personal protective equipment

(1)   Every employer shall ensure that suitable personal protective equipment is provided to his employees who may be exposed to a risk to their health or safety while at work except where and to the extent that such risk has been adequately controlled by other means which are equally or more effective.

(2)   Every self-employed person shall ensure that he is provided with suitable personal protective equipment where he may be exposed to a risk to his health or safety while at work except where and to the extent that such risk has been adequately controlled by other means which are equally or more effective.

(3) Without prejudice to the generality of paragraphs (1) and (2), personal protective equipment shall not be suitable unless -

(a) it is appropriate for the risk or risks involved and the conditions at the place where exposure to the risk may occur;

(b) it takes account of ergonomic requirements and the state of health of the person or persons who may wear it;

(c) it is capable of fitting the wearer correctly, if necessary, after adjustments within the range for which it is designed;

(d) so far as is practicable, it is effective to prevent or adequately control the risk or risks involved without increasing overall risk;

(e) it complies with any enactment (whether in an Act or instrument) which implements in Great Britain any provision on design or manufacture with respect to health or safety in any relevant Community directive listed in Schedule 1 which is applicable to that item of personal protective equipment.

Maintenance and replacement of personal protective equipment

(1) Every employer shall ensure that any personal protective equipment provided to his employees is maintained (including replaced or cleaned as appropriate) in an efficient state, in efficient working order and in good repair.

(2) Every self-employed person shall ensure that any personal protective equipment provided to him is maintained (including replaced or cleaned as appropriate) in an efficient state, in efficient working order and in good repair.

Control of Substances Hazardous to Health Regulations 1994

Prevention or control of exposure to substances hazardous to health

(5) Any personal protective equipment provided by an employer in pursuance of this regulation shall comply with any enactment (whether in an Act or instrument) which implements in Great Britain any provision on design or manufacture with respect to health or safety in any relevant Community directive listed in Schedule 1 to the Personal Protective Equipment at Work Regulations 1992 which is applicable to that item of personal protective equipment.

(8) Where respiratory protective equipment is provided in pursuance of this regulation, than it shall -

(a) be suitable for the purpose; and

(b) comply with paragraph (5) or, where no requirement is imposed by virtue of that paragraph, be of a type approved or shall conform to a standard approved, in either case, by the Executive.

Suitability of work equipment

(1)   Every employer shall ensure that work equipment is so constructed or adapted as to be suitable for the purpose for which it is used or provided.

(2)   In selecting work equipment, every employer shall have regard to the working conditions and to the risks to the health and safety of persons which exist in the premises or undertaking in which that work equipment is to be used and any additional risk posed by the use of that work equipment.

(3)   Every employer shall ensure that work equipment is used only for operations for which, and under conditions for which, it is suitable.

(4)   In this regulation "suitable" means suitable in any respect which it is reasonably foreseeable will affect the health or safety of any person.

Maintenance

(1)   Every employer shall ensure that work equipment is maintained in an efficient state, in efficient working order and in good repair.

Standards relevant to manholes and other access to confined spaces

The following Standards are relevant:

- BS 8007:1987 *Design of concrete structures for retaining aqueous fluids.* Code of practice. Minimum openings specified as 600 mm x 900 mm;

- *Silos UK: Draft design code for silos, bins, bunkers and hoppers,* published by BSI in association with the British Materials Handling Board, gives the minimum as 600 mm x 600 mm;

- BS 5502: Part 50 1993: *Code of practice for design, construction and use of storage tanks and reception pits for livestock slurry* gives access hatches etc as not less than 600 mm x 600 mm;

- BS 8005: *Sewerage* Part 1 1987 *Guide to new sewerage construction* gives the minimum clear opening dimension for manholes for drainage purposes as 600 mm x 600 mm for sewers less than 1 m diameter, except for very shallow manholes where this dimension may be 550 mm;

- BS ISO 9669:1990 *Series 1 freight containers. Interface connections for tank containers.*

References and further guidance

A guide to the Health and Safety at Work etc Act 1974 5th ed L1 HSE Books 1992 ISBN 0 7176 0441 1

Management of health and safety at work Approved Code of Practice L21 HSE Books 1992 ISBN 0 7176 0412 8

Workplace health, safety and welfare Approved Code of Practice and guidance on regulations L24 HSE Books 1992 ISBN 0 7176 0413 6

Work equipment Guidance on regulations L22 HSE Books 1992 ISBN 0 7176 0414 4

Personal protective equipment at work Guidance on regulations L25 HSE Books 1992 ISBN 0 7176 0415 2

Memorandum of Guidance on the Electricity at Work Regulations 1989 HSR25 HSE Books 1989 ISBN 0 11 883963 2

Diving operations at work Guidance on regulations (Regulations and guidance currently being revised)

The management and administration of safety and health at mines. Management and Administration of Safety and Health at Mines Regulations 1993 Approved Code of Practice L44 HSE Books 1993 ISBN 0 7176 0618 X

General COSHH ACOP (control of substances hazardous to health) and carcinogens ACOP (control of carconogenic substances) and biological agents ACOP (control of biological agents) Control of Substances Hazardous to Health Regulations 1994 Approved Code of Practice L5 HSE Books 1997 ISBN 0 7176 1308 9

Noise at work: noise assessment, information and control. Noise guides 3-8 HSG56 HSE Books 1990 ISBN 0 11 885430 5

The control of asbestos at work Approved Code of Practice 2nd ed L27 HSE Books 1993 ISBN 0 11 882037 0

The control of lead at work Approved Code of Practice 2nd rev ed COP2 HSE Books 1996 ISBN 0 7176 1046 2 (currently being revised)

The protection of persons against ionising radiation arising from any work activity Approved Code of Practice L58 HSE Books 1985 ISBN 0 7176 0508 6

A framework for the restriction of occupational exposure to ionising radiation HSG91 HSE Books 1992 ISBN 0 11 886324 X

Managing construction for health and safety Approved Code of Practice L54 HSE Books 1995 ISBN 0 7176 0792 5

Respiratory protective equipment Legislative requirements and lists of HSE approved standards and type approved equipment 4th ed HSE Books 1995 ISBN 0 7176 1036 5 (Many of the items included will be superseded by items bearing the CE marking)

Respiratory protective equipment: a practical guide for users HSG53 HSE Books 1990 ISBN 0 11 885522 0

First aid at work Approved Code of Practice and guidance L74 HSE Books 1997 ISBN 0 7176 1050 0

A guide to information, instruction and training INDG235 HSE Books 1996 Free from HSE Books

5 steps to information, instruction and training INDG213 HSE Books 1996 Free from HSE Books

Guidance on permit-to-work systems in the petroleum industry Oil Industry Advisory Committee guidance booklet 3rd ed HSE Books 1997
 ISBN 0 7176 1281 3

Health and Safety (Safety Signs and Signals) Regulations 1996 SI 1996/341 HSE Books 1996 ISBN 0 11 054093 X

Safety signs and signals Guidance on regulations L64 HSE Books 1996 ISBN 0 7176 0870 0

The future availabilty and currency of the references listed in this publication cannot be guaranteed.

Printed and published by the Health and Safety Executive

C100   9/97